Full-Color Victorian Fashions
1870–1893

Edited and with an Introduction by

JoAnne Olian
Curator Emeritus, Costume Collection
Museum of the City of New York

DOVER PUBLICATIONS, INC.
Mineola, New York

Bibliographical Note

Full-Color Victorian Fashions: 1870–1893 is a new work, first published by Dover Publications, Inc., in 1999.

DOVER *Pictorial Archive* SERIES

Library of Congress Cataloging-in-Publication Data

Full-color Victorian fashions, 1870–1893 / edited and with an introduction by JoAnne Olian.
    p.   cm.
  ISBN 0-486-40484-6 (pbk.)
  1. Costume—History—19th   century. 2. Fashion—History—19th   century.
I. Olian, JoAnne.
GT595.F85   1999
391'.2'09034—dc21   99-14122
                                                 CIP

Manufactured in the United States of America
Dover Publications, Inc., 31 East 2nd Street, Mineola, N.Y. 11501

INTRODUCTION

The ancestors of today's fashion magazines are to be found among the costume books of the 16th century—the first one published, predictably enough, in Paris, in 1562. These early volumes were actually geographies depicting charming, often naive, and sometimes even imagined clothing worn in the newly discovered lands of the Old and New World. They were also compilations of traditional European costume, peasant garb, occupational dress, and apparel decreed by the sumptuary laws, which sought to distinguish various strata of society for the purpose of limiting private expenditures for goods such as clothing. However, it was not until the latter part of the 18th century that the modern fashion journal was conceived, whose purpose was to present the latest styles fresh from the weavers and dressmakers of Paris to an avid public. Then, by the middle of the 19th century, a growing middle class joined the ranks of privileged society in demanding and receiving virtually instantaneous information about novelties in dress and accessories which seemed to materialize by the hour. To a contemporary observer, it appeared that "fashion publications abound today. Descriptions, history, practical details, information à propos the toilette, nothing is lacking to help women fulfill their fantasies. An army of sources endeavors daily to concoct a multiplicity of adjuncts to beauty" (Augustin Challamel, *Histoire de la Mode in France*, 1875).

To be "comme il faut" was extraordinarily time-consuming simply because of the number and variety of activities that demanded changes in costume, creating unprecedented opportunities for the fashion artist as well as the dressmaker. In 1866, a French observer enumerated the sartorial requisites: "A society woman who wants to be well dressed for all occasions at all times needs at least seven or eight toilettes per day: a morning dressing gown, a riding outfit, an elegant simple gown for lunch, a day dress if walking, an afternoon dress for visiting by carriage, a smart outfit to drive through the Bois de Boulogne, a gown for dinner, and a gala dress for evening or the theater." (Henri Despaigne, *Le Code de la Mode*, Paris, 1866) The bourgeoise ardently desired to appear comme il faut, imitating fashionable society by studying the dictates of haute couture, every nuance of which was unveiled in fashion journals. Hence, it was "necessary that information relative to the creation of costumes be reported to the public. This information [was] disseminated by a specialized press: the fashion press" (Bruno du Roselle, *La Mode*, Paris, 1980).

The golden age of the fashion plate is considered to be from 1840 to 1870, when approximately 100 fashion magazines were spawned, the majority of them French. Most were weeklies that also published fiction, household hints, and instructions for parlor pastimes, but all of them reported the latest fashion foibles. They featured at least one black-and-white fashion plate containing several figures, while usually including a hand-colored engraving of two or three ladies, often accompanied by a child.

Since France was the undisputed capital of fashion, many American periodicals made arrangements with their foreign counterparts in order to publish their plates. Among the longest lived of the French fashion journals were *La Mode Illustrée*, introduced in 1860, and *Le Journal des Demoiselles*, which first appeared in 1833 (finally merging with the *Petit Courrier des Dames* toward the century's end), both of which endured well into the 20th century. The former was geared to the provincial housewife and offered much practical advice. It never aspired to the level of chic found in *Le Journal des Demoiselles*, which owed its longevity partly to the fact that it continued to publish hand-colored engravings long after most other magazines had succumbed to color lithographs of inferior quality.

French fashion was so dominant by mid-century that during the Franco-Prussian War, when Paris was under siege and communication with the outside world was cut off, foreign magazines were forced to publish—with apologies—their own inferior black-and-white plates. The French, while unable to export their engravings, continued to publish undaunted and attempted to send the latest fashion news via balloon and carrier pigeon within their country's borders.

Nineteenth-century Paris was devoted to the depiction of women both on canvas and on the printed page. The fashionable Parisienne was a favorite subject of such artists as Ingres, Tissot, Boudin, and Béraud. While their canvases are often stylish renditions of women elegantly garbed, promotion of the latest couture was certainly *not* their intention. Indeed, the subjects wore apparel from their personal wardrobes, or rented by the artist from a couturier. Nonetheless, the line between art and fashion became blurred, particularly with regard to portraiture, while paintings of genre scenes not unlike those depicted in fashion plates were also popular with visitors to the Salons. Monet and Cézanne even went so far as to copy the style of fashion plates, sometimes replicating both composition and dress. Émile Zola referred to such canvases with contempt, calling them "fashion prints": "If your painting is as flat as a coloured engraving in the *Magasin des Demoiselles*, and if your figures look like cardboard dummies dressed by Worth, your success will know no bounds."

Fashion illustration was undeniably a minor art form, borne out by surviving examples of the original watercolor paintings from which the engravings were made. Most artists signed their plates and worked exclusively for one or two publications. One of the finest of these illustrators was Jules David (1808–1892), whose plates from *Le Moniteur des Dames et des Demoiselles* from 1870 to 1878, appear in this book. He studied painting with a pupil of the celebrated Jacques Louis David. He first exhibited in the Paris Salon of 1834, and was also a well-known book illustrator. For fifty years, until his death, he drew all the plates for *Le Moniteur de la Mode*. His work also appeared in other French journals including the aforementioned *Moniteur des Dames et des Demoiselles*, which ceased publication after 1878, as well as in such journals abroad as the *Englishwoman's Domestic Magazine*. Several other artists of David's caliber, including E. Preval, also drew for *Le Moniteur des Dames*. The post-1878 illustrations in this book are from *Le Journal des Demoiselles*, and are signed by both the artist and the engraver on the original plates. (Some of the signatures are discernible on these pages.)

Fashion plates, in addition to depicting the latest styles, were also conversation pieces reflecting an idealized version of the atmosphere in which society moved. They were stylizations of the current standard of beauty, as well as a chronicle of the pastimes of the era. Ladies were portrayed in settings evocative of a world where it was always fair, the temperature moderate, with never more than a gentle breeze, where beautifully behaved children never rumpled their clothes or spilled their cocoa. Here women were perennially young, their coiffures always perfect; and they were never anything but the ideal size and shape for the silhouette of a particular time. It was a world without men, and yet there was no dearth of appealing children of both sexes, gotten up in beautifully detailed miniature versions of the mode.

Dressed in their finery, with no more expression on their serene faces than an occasional half-smile, these ladies turn an untroubled gaze onto nothing in particular wherever the artist decides to place them. Not a flicker of emotion shows on their faces whether they find themselves in the country, at the shore, shopping in town, paying calls, or receiving visitors at home in impeccably furnished interiors. Blissfully oblivious to the labor involved in the intricate sewing of their clothes, and the elaborate care required to maintain them, they make their appearance turned out in heedless elegance.

The ideal of beauty underwent a dramatic metamorphosis between 1870 and 1893: i.e., from the delicate Dresden figurine to the "seven foot beauty with the ten inch waist"—the statuesque Gibson Girl. Dressing fashionably requires a measure of creativity, and with the mute complicity of the fashion illustrator, women reinvent themselves as styles change. Not only do modes of dress vary, but the fashionable body itself undergoes constant transformation. In the 19th century, it was primarily the corset that made it possible to achieve an approximation of the ideal current armature, as decreed by the fashion plate.

The 1870s ushered in a period of extremely feminine and elaborate styles with short waists, sloping shoulders, and puffy bustles. From hair to hem, everything was crimped, looped, puffed and adorned with flounces, flowers, ribbons and bows in the style of Mme. Pompadour and the filmy fichus of the exiled Empress Eugenie's idol, Marie Antoinette (Plates 6 and 7). As the decade progressed, the silhouette smoothed out somewhat and the torso elongated (Plate 17). By 1878, the bustle had vanished and the body was encased in an armor-like sheath which owed its success to the corsets which supported it, and severely tailored costumes made their appearance (Plate 22).

The pencil-slim silhouette began to round at the hips and thrust backward again in 1882 (Plates 24 and 28), in a reprise of the bustle of the seventies, reaching its most exaggerated form by mid-decade, and subsiding only at its end. The eighties version of the bustle was higher and squarer than its predecessor, and in some illustrations it appears almost possible to balance a teacup on it (Plates 37 and 38). The emphasis shift-ed to the sleeves in the nineties, as the shoulder puff inflated until the fullness culminated in enormous melon or leg-of-mutton sleeves (Plates 50 and 51).

Fashion plates are unerring barometers of social change. A comparison between the first and last images in this book reveals much about the metamorphosis of women which took place between 1870 and 1893. The modest demeanor of the demure ladies peering at the angelic baby asleep in its draped cradle (Plate 1) contrasts dramatically with the insouciant bearing of the 1893 beauty who leans against a mantelpiece on her elbow, her weight on one hip (Plate 52). Her gown is infinitely more revealing, diaphanous and sophisticated than a lady would have considered proper twenty years earlier, and her gaze is straightforward amd candid. She is undeniably a self-possessed modern woman who ably stands alone, and for whom the need to share the page with another woman or a child is clearly superfluous. Such an up-to-date creature would undoubtedly have found the photographs which were beginning to encroach on the hand-colored engravings in her fashion journals more to her turn-of-the-century taste than the charming, slightly quaint illustrations of the previous generation of artists.

From Franz Winterhalter to John Singer Sargent, Jules David to Charles Dana Gibson, there was an extraordinary transformation of the fashionable ideal that must be viewed in the context of the enormous social and technological changes which took place in the last quarter of the 19th century. While models in the early years of fashion photography appeared heavy and wooden, and did nothing to enhance the clothes, their presence nonetheless marked the beginning of a new era in fashion journalism that remains unbroken to the present day.

Fashion illustration is rarely to be seen in today's magazines. The photographer's model has replaced the drawing by diligently molding herself into the embodiment of the attenuated, impossibly slim and tall creature conceived by the fashion artist. Instead of merely gazing into a flattering mirror and beholding an idealized reflection, she has transformed herself and merged with the illusion, becoming the vision of reality delighted in by the camera.

JoAnne Olian

New York City
November 1998

NOTES ON THE PLATES

(These notes have been translated from the original French descriptions—where available; for some of the more obscure French fashion terms, brief, general definitions have been added parenthetically.)

From *Le Moniteur des Dames et des Demoiselles*, 1870–78

PLATE 1. FALL 1870
Dressy toilettes: Mme. Du Riez. Ribbons and passementerie: A la Ville de Lyon.

PLATE 2. DECEMBER 1870
LEFT: Little girl of eight to ten in dress of plaid poplin, with sleeveless pardessus of velvet and plaid sash. CENTER: At home toilette with lace Maintenon coiffure, falling in barbes in the back. Trimmed with fringe, the jacket of embroidered velvet falls narrow and square in front, long and bouffant in back. The Venetian sleeves are lined with satin, and the satin dress is trimmed with two flounces with turned-up headings. RIGHT: Dressy toilette for dinner or "little" evenings. Satin Watteau bow in the hair. Faille dress—with satin piping and black lace ruffle trim—has a high-necked corsage (bodice) with slightly full sleeves, and a flat-fronted skirt with a train, no pouf in back.

PLATE 3. NOVEMBER–DECEMBER 1870
LEFT: Toilette for young lady with blue velvet chapeau perched on the forehead, adorned with grey feathers and taffeta ribbons. Blue velvet dress trimmed with grey squirrel has a high-necked corsage—fitted at the waist—ending in a basque with cut-out tabs. The short skirt, trimmed with bands of grey squirrel, is topped by velvet ruches. CENTER: Toilette for little girl of eight to ten with black velvet toque, trimmed with black and red feathers. Dress and belt of plaid taffeta, with sleeveless corsage and bunched-up tunic of black velvet. RIGHT: Dressy town toilette with pouf chapeau in black velvet, trimmed with a pansy satin ruche (edging), strings, and matching feathers. High-necked black velvet dress with demi-full sleeves and plain skirt. Sleeveless Watteau pardessus of pansy velvet, fitted at the waist with a belt, and edged with a band of marten.

PLATE 4. MAY–JUNE 1871
Summer toilettes: Mme. Du Riez. Child's costume: Au Cardinal Fesch. Ribbons and passementerie: A la Ville de Lyon.

PLATE 5. SUMMER 1871
Promenade toilettes. LEFT: Toilette for a girl of ten with rice straw chapeau, high crown, curled-up brim faced in taffeta, and taffeta bow. Sleeveless jacket and skirt of plaid taffeta, with poplin tunic, and buttons and belt of velvet. CENTER: Italian straw chapeau with a high crown and wide brim, edged in black velvet, and trimmed with crepe de chine and a sprig of geranium. Chignon falling very low and lightly waved. Moblot (military style) jacket, trimmed with a buttoned flap in back, forming two wide pleats to the waist in silk serge, with collar, revers, piped edges, epaulets, and cuffs of taffeta. Dress of finely striped taffeta: first skirt straight, cut-out hem edged with a ruffle; second skirt trimmed with five ruffles. RIGHT: Straw chapeau, with white tulle underneath, trimmed with taffeta ribbons, flowers, and a single white bird's wing. Dress of ecru toile, redingote corsage, with capelet crossed in front; large basques opening to revers in front, split in back, and edged with piping and a ruffle. Large pockets on each side, and solid, slightly long skirt.

PLATE 6. SUMMER 1871
Promenade toilettes: Mme. Herst. Ribbons and passementerie: A la Ville de Lyon. Lace: Violard Frères. LEFT: Lamballe costume includes chapeau of rice straw trimmed with beautiful, wide white ostrich plumes, taffeta bows, and trailing greenery. India muslin fichu embroidered with large dots, and adorned with a taffeta bow. Black-striped dress of droguet (mixed wool fabric) with low-necked corsage and bias sleeves. Skirt with demi-train, and deep bias flounce to hem.

Embroidered muslin cuff falling over the hand. RIGHT: Round chapeau of Italian straw decorated with a single rose and a feather, and trimmed with black velvet. Low neck Indies foulard dress with lace-trimmed fichu and velvet bow. Sleeves widen toward wrist. Fitted, slightly open basquine (jacket). Flounces to the floor trim the tunic skirt and the second skirt.

PLATE 7. MAY 1871
LEFT: Dressy toilette for a young person starts with a coiffure adorned with a chaperon and cornflowers. Dress in tarlatan or white mousseline, with lavalière bows of taffeta ribbon. CENTER: Walking toilette includes chapeau Berrichon of English straw edged with black velvet, trimmed with a white tulle ruche and a rose. Printed mousseline dress. RIGHT: Five-year-old girl with a velvet ribbon in her hair. White mousseline guimpe (chemisette). Taffeta dress with a ruffle on the bodice, and skirt ruffles applied in half-circles.

PLATE 8. MARCH 1871
LEFT: Little girl of ten or eleven wears an Eva coiffure adorned with a bunch of flowers to one side. Blue taffeta dress trimmed with bows and piping in a deeper shade of blue. Square corsage à la Vierge. Guimpe and sleeves of mousseline with lace. CENTER: Formal dinner or evening toilette begins with a coiffure decorated with forget-me-nots. The faille dress is trimmed with satin piping and facing; guimpe and little sleeves of white crepe. Corsage-tunic with edging; ruffle and bows all piped with satin. The tunic skirt is open in front, raised at each side by a bow, ending in back with a beautiful, wide folded pleat faced in satin. The second skirt is short in front, very long in back with a train, and trimmed all around with two rows of piping and two bows on each side, ending in a ruffle. The underskirt is short in front, long in back. RIGHT: Walking toilette with a chapeau Louis XV, composed of a tiny brim covered with velvet bows, a rose, buds, and leaves; pretty bow with ends in back, lace strings. Faille dress with appliquéd trim of black velvet and black lace. Corsage forming a high-necked basquine, simulating a waistcoat in front between longer basques on each side. Sleeves fitted on top, wide at the base. Second skirt has square flaps of two lengths, trimmed like the basquine. Solid skirt with hem just to the floor.

PLATE 9. DECEMBER 1874
Evening toilettes: Mme. Morison. Ribbons and passementerie: A la Ville de Lyon. LEFT: Costume for ten year old girl. White taffeta dress, princesse style in front, where the skirt is trimmed with a pale blue taffeta flounce, surmounted by two smaller white taffeta flounces with a blue bow on the side. The same skirt, with a ruffle at the hem in back, forms a modest pouf above, supported by blue ribbons tied in a bow in the center; a ribbon coming from the bow is attached at the shoulder. Low-necked square corsage is framed by a mousseline bouillonné (shirred band of fabric). CENTER: Toilette in two shades of reseda green. The trained skirt is of dark faille, solid in back, trimmed at the hem in front with a yellow piping, topped by two rows of pale faille pleats, headed with a chicoree ruche ("pinked" edging) of pale faille with yellow edging. A faille tablier (apron) crosses the front of the petticoat diagonally—attached at the hem—and forms a bow, a wide tail and a scallop, all with dark faille piping, fringes and matching ball fringe, and yellow binding. In back, the petticoat covers a long yellow pouf, framed on each side by wide tails of dark green, trimmed with piping and ball fringe. Low-necked cuirasse corsage (tight, boned bodice), long in front, with little basques in back, is composed of two shades of faille, trimmed with yellow fringe and piping; bow and roses in the center. Very short puffed sleeve, edged with

white lace. In the hair, a bunch of roses similar to those on the dress, and a pale green feather. RIGHT: Costume of soft pink taffeta for a young lady. The trained skirt is puffed in front and striped with puffed, tubular bands. In back, it is encircled by two flounces, headed by two rows of puffed bands, a pouf, and a ruche. A simple bow with floating ends joins the pouf in the center. Low-necked corsage, rounded point in front and postillion back, trimmed with shoulder straps. Tiny puffed sleeves. Velvet bow and rosebuds in the hair.

PLATE 10. NOVEMBER 1874

Dresses: Mlle. Koenig. Town toilettes. LEFT: Costume of black cashmere and faille. Petticoat, with cashmere train, encircled by two rows of ruffles, and a third one only in the back. Cashmere tablier, attached in back by faille loops, and trimmed with two rows of ruffles. The corsage, of cashmere, has an embroidered plastron (V-shaped front), and is edged with faille and cashmere pleats. Black felt chapeau, turned up brim, trimmed with chestnut faille and tobacco-colored plumes. RIGHT: Costume in limousine (twilled herringbone worsted), with fine, faded multi-color stripes on a grey ground. Barely noticeable train encircled by wide bias bands applied like flounces and ending in a netted fringe of matching wool. Polonaise blouse, forming a long tablier and raised in back; the edges are trimmed with bias and fringe. Mantelet (tailored shawl) of a new type, in the same fabric; high neck and collar of fringe, ending in a bow in front. The ends of this mantelet are as wide as the tunic fronts, and the sides, draped, fasten in back under a passementerie motif. Matching fringes on all edges. Black felt chapeau, velvet bow, and acacia branches.

PLATE 11. JUNE 1875

Walking toilettes. LEFT: Blue taffeta petticoat with short train, flat pleats in front, alternating gathered and pleated flounces in back, headed by two puffs, with ruched headings. Grey foulard tunic with blue stripes, edged with blue taffeta bias bands. Foulard corsage, small flat basques, blue taffeta collar, cuffs, buttons, and trim. Batiste lingerie trim with lace. Rice straw chapeau, turned-up brim faced with black velvet and trimmed with a blue ribbon butterfly bow, and a branch of pink acacia. RIGHT: Costume of reseda wool armure (pebbly-surfaced fabric). Petticoat skimming the ground encircled by a pleated flounce, very high in back, where it is topped by a bias ribbon of light faille. Two small pleated flounces, edged with pale reseda, delineate the bottom of the tablier, and are attached on each side with matching bows. Tunic-sash in pale reseda, raised in back. Open shawl collar corsage with long square basques in front, short ones in back, matching ribbon trim. Flat pleats with a ruche edge the neck and sleeves. Lingerie trim of pleated mousseline. English straw chapeau encircled with a black ribbon and adorned with roses.

PLATE 12. JUNE 1875

Toilettes for the country. LEFT: Toilette of checked and solid turtledove color toile. Petticoat with short train, encircled by ruched ruffles. Tablier draped and shirred in back, attached by a wide matching ribbon bow. Corsage with square basques in front, postillion back, edged with a ruched ruffle; matching ribbon butterfly bows cascade down the center back. Solid and checked ruffles at wrists. Lingerie trim of ruched batiste and lace. Chapeau of Italian straw, turned-back brim faced in bright pink faille; roses in front and ribbon bow in back. Pink ribbon around the crown, a bunch of Bengal roses on top and on the bottom in back. RIGHT: Suit of grey toile. Petticoat with short train, encircled by vertical bands of black braid, mother-of-pearl button trim. Polonaise with basques under the belt; black braid on all the edges of the garment, mother-of-pearl button closing. Toile strap edged with black braid, supporting a kind of gamebag hanging from the basque in back. Lingerie trim of embroidered toile. Black straw chapeau, brim faced with grey faille to match the toilette. Bunch of daisies under and above the brim, with a brown bird's wing holding a floating veil of blue gauze.

PLATE 13. MAY 1875

Toilettes for the country. LEFT: Toilette of grey wool and silk, and black faille. A ruffle topped by a roll is near the train; grey pleats trim the skirt. The tunic, made like a pointed tablier, has a black faille border. A grey scarf passes through large eyelets and ends in a bow. The tunic, slightly longer in back, is lifted gracefully on the side. Cuirass corsage and sleeves are trimmed with black piping. Medici collar. Chapeau of English straw, trimmed with black velvet and daisies mixed with other flowers. RIGHT: Dress of blue faille and crepeline.

The faille skirt is completely pleated in back. The front shirring is crepeline. The garment, a tunic, is of embroidered crepeline. The front is one piece. The sleeve consists of a kind of capelet attached in back, leaving the arms free. Rich matching fringe. Faille chapeau trimmed with Belgian straw. Spray of roses in several shades on the brim. Underneath, a faille bow.

PLATE 14. JANUARY 1875

Town toilettes. LEFT: Dress in bottle-green wool. Skirt has a slight train, wide pleats in front, with two scarves crossing in the center. The sides, which project over the tablier, are trimmed with a Greek motif of black wool braid, to the hem. The cuirass corsage is trimmed with a smaller version of the same motif. Demi-fitted paletot in hazelnut duvetyn (twill weave with velvet-like finish), is trimmed with sable and fancy buttons. Chapeau of brown felt with matching velvet ribbons, and a bird's wing of several shades on one side. RIGHT: Suit of black velvet and iron grey faille. Velvet skirt with slight train, rising to the belt in back with pleats à la religieuse. The tablier is grey faille, shirred crosswise, and separated from five small flounces by black velvet with points and bows. Velvet Louis XIV corsage with long flat basques. The front is trimmed like the tablier. High, flared collar of velvet faced with faille. Lingerie trim of batiste and ruched lace. Black velvet chapeau, trimmed with a torsade (twist) of blue velvet, bow on the side; a black feather is perched on top with panache.

PLATE 15. OCTOBER 1875

Promenade toilettes. LEFT: Suit of Russia leather color sicilienne (ribbed silk and wool) and faille. Petticoat with short train, forming a pouf at the top; a pleated ruffle at the hem, topped by black braid stripes with jet embroidery. Very short tablier ending with similar trim, whose sides disappear under the pouf. Jacket-style corsage, completely striped with braid. Turned-down collar and sleeves of faille; braid striped cuffs and ribbon bow. Embroidered lingerie trim. Chapeau of velvet to match the dress, topped with a cluster of black feathers. RIGHT: Suit of pearl-grey cashmere, plain and checked with tobacco and grey. Petticoat with short train and Bulgarian pleat of tobacco faille, trimmed with little gathered ruffles. Tablier striped with wide bands of tobacco faille and bordered with plain cashmere pleats. The tablier ties in back with a wide tobacco ribbon. New style corsage, striped with tobacco bands, in front; the back is covered by a capelet from the shoulder seams. Pleated lingerie trim. Felt chapeau with soft grey cashmere crown, encircled by a tobacco ribbon tied on top. Comb and matching headband of garden flowers.

PLATE 16. NOVEMBER 1877

Visiting and reception toilettes: Mme. Breant-Castel. LEFT: Suit of mauve faille and black wool. Princesse dress in faille, a pleated ruffle at the hem, emphasized by a double-scalloped band outlined in black. Grand paletot of black Indies wool, semi-fitted, and closed on the diagonal. All the edges are piped in mauve. The very original pocket design is composed of three triangles, superimposed on a piece of faille. Triple collar. Pleated nainsook (thin, delicate cotton) lingerie trim. Black satin bonnet with a soft crown and a diadem brim. Black velvet ribbon around the crown, mauve feathers; velvet drapery on the front of the brim. RIGHT: Velvet suit of moss green velvet in a somber shade, and matching faille in a lighter tone. Plain velvet petticoat. Long corsage of alternating velvet and faille. Frogs of silk cord trim the sleeves and serve as the front closure. A faille tunic encircles the bottom of the corsage, and is folded over to form the tablier; the two ends are simply tied in back, falling over the train. Rich silk fringe matches both shades of the suit. Fluted crepe lingerie trim.

PLATE 17. DECEMBER 1877

Ball toilettes. LEFT: Princesse costume in white faille and pompadour brocade with a pink ground. The front forms both a square-necked faille waistcoat and a petticoat tablier. A pleated blue faille ruffle trims the hem of the tablier, which has white faille scarves that disappear under the court manteau. The lower scarf is trimmed with a pleated pink faille ruffle, pink and blue pleats above, held at center front. The second scarf has a ruffle only on the bottom, trimmed with a white silk ruffle, embroidered and scalloped with pink. The top trim consists of blue and pink pleats and an embroidered ruffle. The court mantle, an integral part of the toilette, is of pompadour brocade, outlined in pink and blue. The back of the princesse style mantle ends with an added train of fan-shaped layers of pink and blue faille. A blue faille insertion frames the neckline, with a pink faille ruffle;

white crepe Medici collar and sleeve trim. A scalloped, embroidered silk ruffle forms a turned-down collar and trims the sleeves. White lace mitts. Cluster of garden flowers in the hair, attached with a blue bow. RIGHT: Costume of white satin and gauze. Pleated gauze ruffles at the hem, under a cut-out band with satin piping, draped gauze above. The rest of the tablier is trimmed with pleated gauze ruffles. Gauze tunic with jagged edges, piped with satin and marabou fringe. Satin cuirasse covered in gauze with a garland of embroidered and cut-out foliage at the bottom. The corsage is high in back and very low in front where it is trimmed with a modesty-piece of shirred crepe. Gauze fichu edged with pleating and trimmed with a collarette of English blonde lace. A garland of wild roses and leaves attaches the fichu, and crosses the front of the toilette diagonally, ending on the side of the tunic. Short puffed sleeves with blonde lace. Roses on the shoulders and in the hair.

PLATE 18. AUGUST 1878
Toilettes for the country. LEFT: Costume of pink zephyr (lightweight sheer). Petticoat with short train, pleated hem flounce. Princesse style polonaise, the center back completely pleated, widening and slightly puffed at the bottom, framed by a broderie anglaise (eyelet embroidery) ruffle. An insert of the same embroidery with a similar ruffle forms the collar and descends down the center front. The sleeves are trimmed with pink pleats emphasized by embroidery. Lingerie trim of shirred India muslin. Circlet of Italian straw, white facing, encircled by a garland of mauve roses, tied in back with a matching ribbon bow. Pink parasol, lined in white and edged with a black lace ruffle. CENTER: Costume of clear blue toile, for a little girl of four to six. Princesse style, a pleated flounce with an embroidered white band at the hem. A sash, edged with embroidery and divided by a matching insertion, forms a wide pleat below the waist, ending in a bow in back. Two rows of insertions trim the front and flank tiny mother-of-pearl buttons. Insertions and an embroidered ruffle trim the cuffs. Wide embroidered sailor collar. Wavy straw chapeau, Chinese style, trimmed with cornflowers and matching ribbon. RIGHT: Costume of grey-violet zephyr, with white and navy blue stripes. Short petticoat, pleated flounce at the hem. Tunic (or second skirt) tucked up in "washerwoman" style in front, with puff and panel descending in back. Navy blue piping outlines the top edge of broderie anglaise ruffles. "Baby" corsage, pleated front and back, mounted on a yoke. Little capelet of the same fabric, trimmed with blue bands and embroidery, blue pleats at the top. Blue ribbon belt. Lingerie trim of mousseline. English straw chapeau with brim low in front and lifted in back. White silk facing and ruche. Navy blue ribbon around the crown, wide bow in back.

PLATE 19. AUGUST 1878
Toilettes for the casino. LEFT: Costume of linen striped in blue, white, grey, and tobacco for a young lady of eighteen. Short petticoat and attached corsage, completely covered with small pleats. A lace flounce at the hem; a frill of the same lace descends the entire front of the dress, with bunches of matching ribbon. Linen Pierrot collar with a bow. Duchesse sleeves, trimmed with a ribbon band and bow. Round ribbon belt, tied in back, with long floating ends in two shades of blue, ending in a wide bow at the side. Round Belgian straw chapeau, with a wreath of field flowers. RIGHT: Princesse costume of pink faille and white mousseline. The dress is faille with a long train and pleated ruffle at the hem. Mousseline overdress. Frill of Valenciennes lace down the center front, flanked by embroidered insertions. Three garnitures of shirred mousseline, set off by lace, adorn the side of the tablier toward the back. The other side is trimmed with flaps of mousseline and lace. A ladder of pink ribbon bows follows the flaps and descends to the hem. The tunic is puffed in back and edged with mousseline enhanced by lace. Duchesse sleeves with an embroidered insertion, gathered ruffle, and ribbon bow. Open shawl collar of mousseline with lace and bow. Rice straw chapeau, diadem brim, with a band of pink silk and white beads; a garland of apple blossoms around the crown, trailing in back. Silk stockings of dawn pink, coutil (sturdy twill-woven cotton) slippers with pink buckles.

PLATE 20. JULY 1878
Toilettes for the seaside. LEFT: Costume of blue linen. Skirt with short train, three finely pleated flounces at the hem. Princesse-style polonaise, trimmed down the center front with a frill of Flemish lace ending a little above the lower edge, which is cut out and bordered in white. The pocket and the sleeves are trimmed with lace ruching and

a band of linen edged in white; matching belt. Ruched lingerie trim and blue cravat. Cabriolet chapeau of English straw, the brim faced with black velvet. White plume around the crown, held on the side by a blue ribbon rosette. RIGHT: Costume of putty-colored barège (open-weave fabric) and garnet faille. Faille petticoat with a flat flounce cut to allow the barège cornets to pass through. Rolls of barège above the flounce. Polonaise of barège, fringe trim on the bottom, closed by a row of garnet buttons. The bottom is draped in regular pleats, and joined in the center by a bunch of red and black ribbons. The bow serves as the point of departure for a fringe-trimmed barège scarf, draped diagonally on the right of the polonaise, ending at center back, under a red ribbon rosette. The tunic, which completes the back of the polonaise, is made of two lengths, one of barège, the other of faille. A panel of faille, trimmed with putty fringes, is placed on the right side, fixed with two rosettes, one in the center and the other lower down. The sleeves are garnet faille with a barège cuff cut out in strips, like the collar. Plain lingerie trim. Straw chapeau, trimmed with garnet and black satin.

PLATE 21. JUNE 1878
Walking toilettes. LEFT: Short costume, in two shades of cashmere and grey blue faille. Petticoat ending at boot-tops. A flounce of grouped pleats separated by faille tabs. Princesse-style polonaise in front, a faille band at the waist. A simulated faille waistcoat forms the middle of the corsage. It is flanked by long revers which become a sailor collar. The center back is composed of a length of faille, shirred horizontally below the waist, and becoming a triple inverted pleat widening toward the hem. Two faille revers on the sides meet in the middle of these pleats, and are joined by a ribbon bow. The cuffs are pleated and trimmed with a faille band and bow. Scalloped lingerie trim. Chapeau of black straw with a pleated bavolet (a bonnet flounce concealing the back of the neck). A blue ribbon, edged in carob, is placed in rosettes and forms the strings. Marabou ruche in back, gilt pins here and there. CENTER: Costume of putty-colored Indian cashmere and carob-colored faille. Petticoat with train, with a ruched hem flounce whose edge is faced with carob faille, and surmounted by a garniture of alternating cashmere and faille. The train is also trimmed with a ruched flounce, faced in carob. The tunic skirt has an independent tablier, draped in regular pleats, fixed at the sides; it is longer in the center than at the sides. Jacket-corsage with faille vestee (decorative front or half vest); the hem of the basque is made of alternating faille and cashmere. Lingerie trim in mousseline and lace. Chapeau of Italian straw. Under the brim, a bandeau of light foliage with red berries. Carob ribbon rosettes on the side of the crown, with putty-colored plumes adorning both sides. A ribbon divides the crown, appearing to form one of the strings. RIGHT: Costume of putty cashmere for a little girl of eleven. Princesse dress with turned-down shawl collar, open rather low in front; this collar, of deep reseda faille, is edged with pale blue faille. Large blue buttons trim the front. The center back is green faille and forms two little flat basques which rest on a ruched flounce of pale blue faille, edged in green. There is a blue faille band at the hem; the back pouf is edged with faille to match both shades. Green faille cuffs edged in blue. Lingerie trim in plain toile. Round hat of wavy straw, in a greenish shade, with a cluster of apple blossoms to one side.

PLATE 22. JANUARY 1878
At home and visiting toilettes. LEFT: Princesse costume in blue wool with white nubs. Pleated hem flounce with a wide heading of tubular shirring. Yoke piped with carob faille forms the top of the corsage both front and back. Faille plastron center back and front, continuing to the hem and flanked by a wide carob piping in front; the back is shirred, and puffed across and lengthwise. A width of nubby wool is pleated in back at the waist under the plastron; it forms the train and simulates the drape on the sides of the dress. The tunic is lightly puffed toward the back, where it is attached to the train. Turned-down collar of carob faille. The sleeve ends in a cone-shaped cuff with a band of carob ribbon. Lingerie trim of embroidered mousseline. CENTER: Costume in wood-colored neigeuse de laine (a soft wool twill with a mottled appearance and an uneven, rough face), with warp-printed effect in otter and white. Princesse petticoat with added short train, somewhat ample and draped. Princesse style polonaise. A single row of buttons closes the front, which separates into two points at the bottom. The polonaise is draped in a pouf in back. Jacket of the same fabric, with a shawl collar, closed with a single button, spreading wide over the front of the polonaise. Double cuffs. Plain toile lin-

PLATE 23. SEPTEMBER 1878

Visiting and reception toilettes. LEFT: Costume of reseda cashmere. Petticoat without train, a deep hem flounce with wide inverted pleats; a matching velvet ribbon passes between each pleat through vertical slits under the heading, ending in a bow. Princesse-style polonaise. The front closes diagonally, and the bottom part forms the first tablier, draped on the hip and attached in back; the crossed part forms a second tablier attached to the first with velvet bows which adorn its ends. The edges of both tabliers and the corsage, around the neck and the cuffs, have slits, allowing a velvet ribbon to be threaded through. Ruched lingerie trim enhanced with lace. Felt chapeau, edged with black velvet, and adorned with a band and drapery of carob velvet with a black feather. CENTER: Costume of otter-colored lightweight wool for a little boy of seven. Short trousers. Straight waistcoat with tiny matching velvet buttons. Open jacket with long velvet shawl collar, side pockets, and velvet trim on sleeves. RIGHT: Costume of black and blue faille. Petticoat with train and pleated ruffles, divided by rolls of the same fabric. Polonaise, with long blue faille lapels piped in buttercup yellow, is completely open over the petticoat from hem to bust in front. Lapel on the right forms a drapery which reaches to the bottom of the polonaise in back. Pleats of blue and buttercup faille support a bouffant which emerges from the seam in the middle. Buttercup cuffs with blue pleats at the wrists. Double faille pleats of both colors around the neck and on the edges of the lapels frame a simulated yellow vestee. Lingerie trim of white lace.

From *Le Journal des Demoiselles,* 1882-93

PLATE 24, JANUARY 1882

Ball toilettes: Milles. Vidal. LEFT: Round skirt of pleated white gauze, with little embroidered gauze ruffles; diamante gauze (net with diamond-shaped mesh) scarf; tablier in front and pouf in back, held up on the side by three bunches of hyacinths. Diamante gauze corsage, fichu neckline with vestee simulated by a garniture of the same embroidered gauze as the skirt; elbow-length sleeves. Watteau comb with hyacinths in the hair. RIGHT: Tablier gathered across the top to the first lace flounce, falling over a pale pink pouf; square train edged with pleating. Brocaded satin corsage, square-necked in front and pointed in back; princesse back ending in two long tails winding over the train, up to a lace scallop at the panniers (fullness or drapery on hips) of the corsage. The neckline is adorned with embroidered lace which descends in back, emphasizing the point; short, lightly draped sleeves. In the hair, a little feather puff with an aigrette (upright tuft of feathers).

PLATE 25, MARCH 1882

Toilettes: Milles. Vidal. LEFT: Hindu cashmere skirt with double row of pleats, draped tunic cut out in wide points and edged with a little pleated ruffle of satin. Pointed corsage, turned-down collar, satin piping. Double point in back splits, allowing for a pouf which reaches to the hem. CENTER: Short costume in garnet satin. A large flounce of black lace falls over the pleated satin hem. The little panniers are edged with beaded fringe over a lace flounce. Pointed corsage of garnet cut (ciselé) velvet; solid vestee with lace revers; lace sleeve trim. RIGHT: Child's costume with band of inverted pleats at hem, topped by small satin pleats. Pleated satin vestee; little paletot of wool with fan-shaped satin flap. In back, the little skirt is interrupted by fan-shaped satin pleats mounted in the seam of the garment; satin pockets and cuffs, rounded at the edges and attached with buttons; round collar.

PLATE 26, MAY 1882

Modes: Mme. Boucherie. Lace: Maison Lefebure Frères. Five spring chapeaux.

PLATE 27, JULY 1882

Toilettes and modes: Magasins de la Scabieuse. Child's costume: M. Lacroix. LEFT: Little boy's suit with smock of ice blue coutil—double-breasted—with small shawl lapels. Broderie anglaise-edged collar and cuffs. CENTER: Dress trimmed at the bottom with scallops of grenadine edged with Spanish lace, and covered in front with little lace ruffles strewn with jet pendants; short tablier, draped, of beaded grenadine. Lace corsage, fichu neckline, draped lace lapels studded with jet pendants; jet buttons. Black lace bonnet with garland of tiny sprays of red ranunculus, half-hidden by lace. RIGHT: Costume of patterned satinet with pleated satin skirt edged with two rows of finely pleated plain satinet; above, a row of pleated printed satinet over which an embroidered white etamine ruffle falls; long tablier, draped, falling in revers on the side, pleated from the top, with an embroidered edging. Turned-down collar of solid satinet; embroidered cuffs. Chapeau of silver straw with tubular facing of satin, topped with a velvet bow and an ombre feather.

PLATE 28, FEBRUARY 1882

Ready-to-wear toilettes: Maison Simon. Modes: Mme. Boucherie. LEFT: Child's costume of reseda cashmere with two wide rows of pleats at the hem, straight, finely pleated vest; pleated back. Large pleated collar, white lace edging and cuffs. Mascotte chapeau of bronze felt, with a bronze plume, and ombre reseda plumes in front. CENTER: Short costume of plush, satin, and vicuna cashmere in Louis XV blue; the plush skirt has four thick rolls of shirred satin, set on pleated satin. Vicuna scarf edged with a roll, held up on one side with a matching cord, emerging in front and ending with two tassels. Corsage with a vestee of lengthwise shirred satin rolls; plush lapels adorned with small metal buttons; princesse back. The flat sides form a single tail with the pouf; plush cuffs. High-crowned felt chapeau; raised brim faced with plush, trimmed with satin rosette and a feather. RIGHT: Ready-to-wear manteau of embossed otter-colored velvet, lined with ruby plush, with a border of chenille fringe mixed with satin ribbons with little balls. Otter passementerie, falling from the shoulders in back, with tassels. Bonnet of pomponnette; a charming new fabric made of tiny pompons; the brim is otter plush, nearly covered by an otter- and ruby-colored feather; ruby plush strings, crossed in back.

PLATE 29, OCTOBER 1887

Toilettes for hunting; Chapeaux. Mme. Gradoz. Mlle. Helena.

PLATE 30, SUMMER 1887

Toilettes for the seashore.

PLATE 31, JULY 1887

Toilettes and Modes: Mme. Pelletier-Vidal. Chapeaux: Mme. Boucherie. LEFT: Corsage with tails of printed foulard, open over a shirred lace chemisette; lapels of cactus ottoman; shirred lace sleeves with jockeys (ruffled epaulets) on the shoulders. Lace skirt and pouf of ottoman. Chapeau of satin straw and twisted braid with shirred lace facing, white feathers, and ribbons. CENTER: Skirt of grey Gobelins moire checked in white. The pleated panels dividing the skirt are of solid voile. The voile tunic is shirred to a lace yoke; the ribbon belt crosses and ties in back. Bonnet of pleated tulle with a crown of taffeta flounces. RIGHT: Child's costume with white lace V-shaped front, intersected by pale blue bands of ribbon that extend to the base of the pale blue surah corsage. Panels of white lace form the sleeves. Pleated skirt. A sash of ribbon and lace encircles the low waist.

PLATE 32, 1887

Toilettes for summer holidays: Mme. Gradoz. Chapeaux: Mlle. Helena.

PLATE 33, SPRING 1887

Promenade toilettes: Mlle. Thirion. Chapeaux: Mme. Boucherie. Child's costume: Mme. Berger.

PLATE 1. FALL 1870

PLATE 2. DECEMBER 1870

PLATE 3. NOVEMBER-DECEMBER 1870

PLATE 4. MAY–JUNE 1871

Plate 5. Summer 1871

PLATE 6. SUMMER 1871

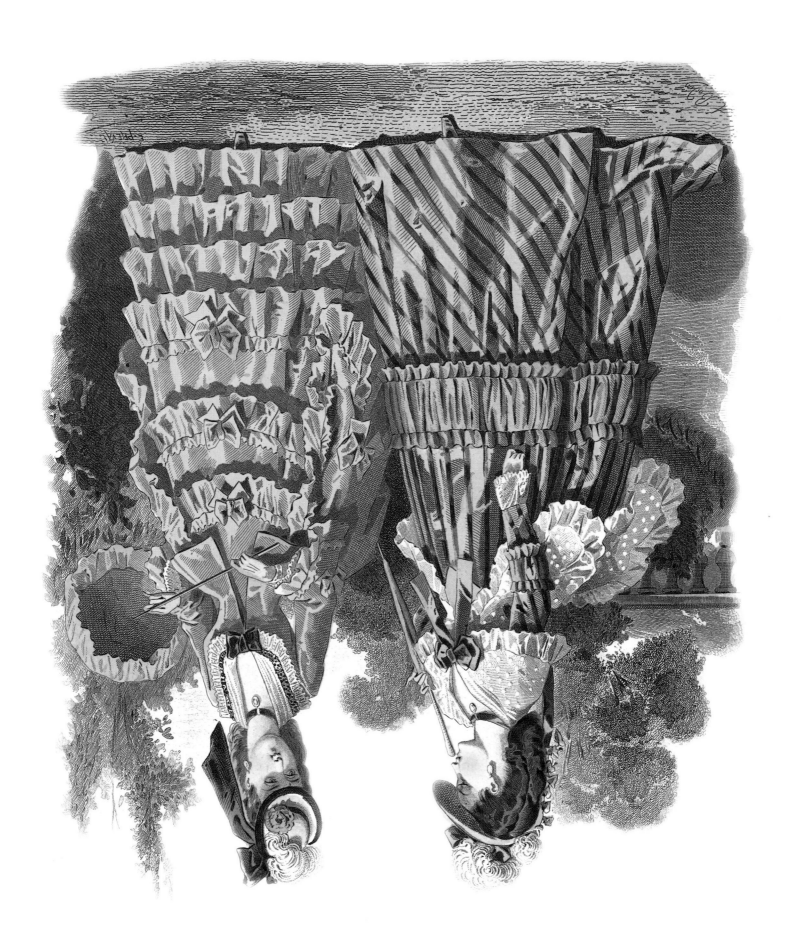

PLATE 7. MAY 1871

PLATE 8. MARCH 1871

PLATE 9. DECEMBER 1874

PLATE 10. NOVEMBER 1874

PLATE 11. JUNE 1875

PLATE 13. MAY 1875

PLATE 15. OCTOBER 1875

PLATE 17. DECEMBER 1877

PLATE 18. AUGUST 1878

PLATE 18. AUGUST 1878

PLATE 19. AUGUST 1878

PLATE 20. July 1878

PLATE 20. July 1878

PLATE 21. JUNE 1878

PLATE 22. JANUARY 1878

PLATE 23. SEPTEMBER 1878

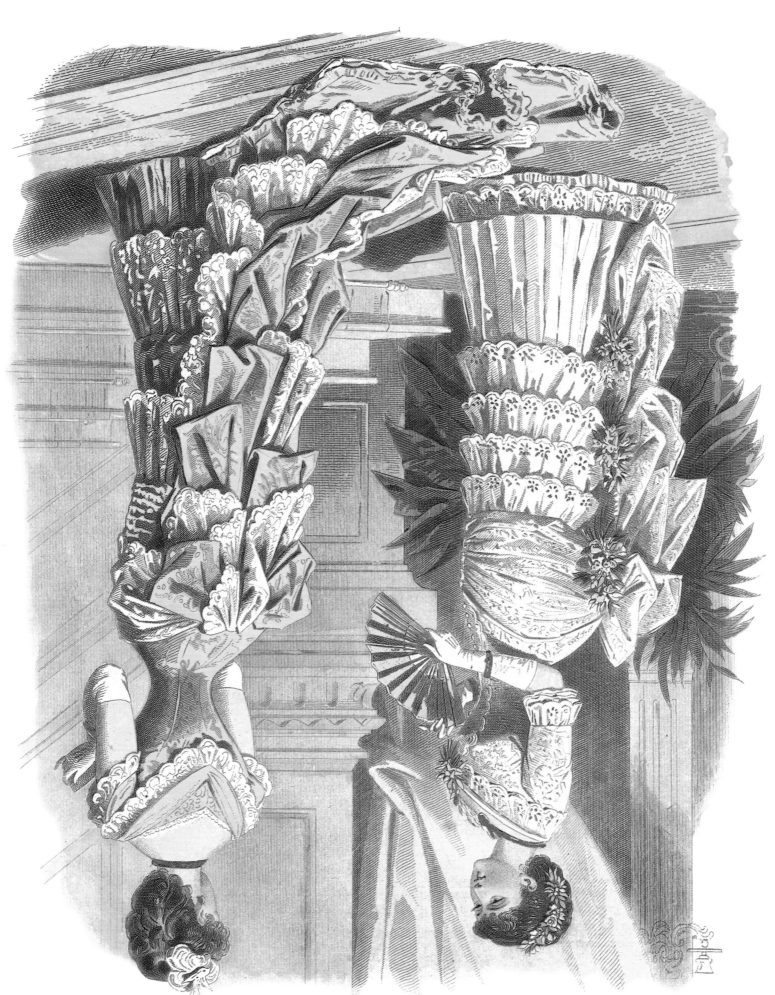

PLATE 25. MARCH 1882

PLATE 26. MAY 1882

PLATE 27. JULY 1882

PLATE 28. FEBRUARY 1882

PLATE 29. OCTOBER 1887

PLATE 30. SUMMER 1887

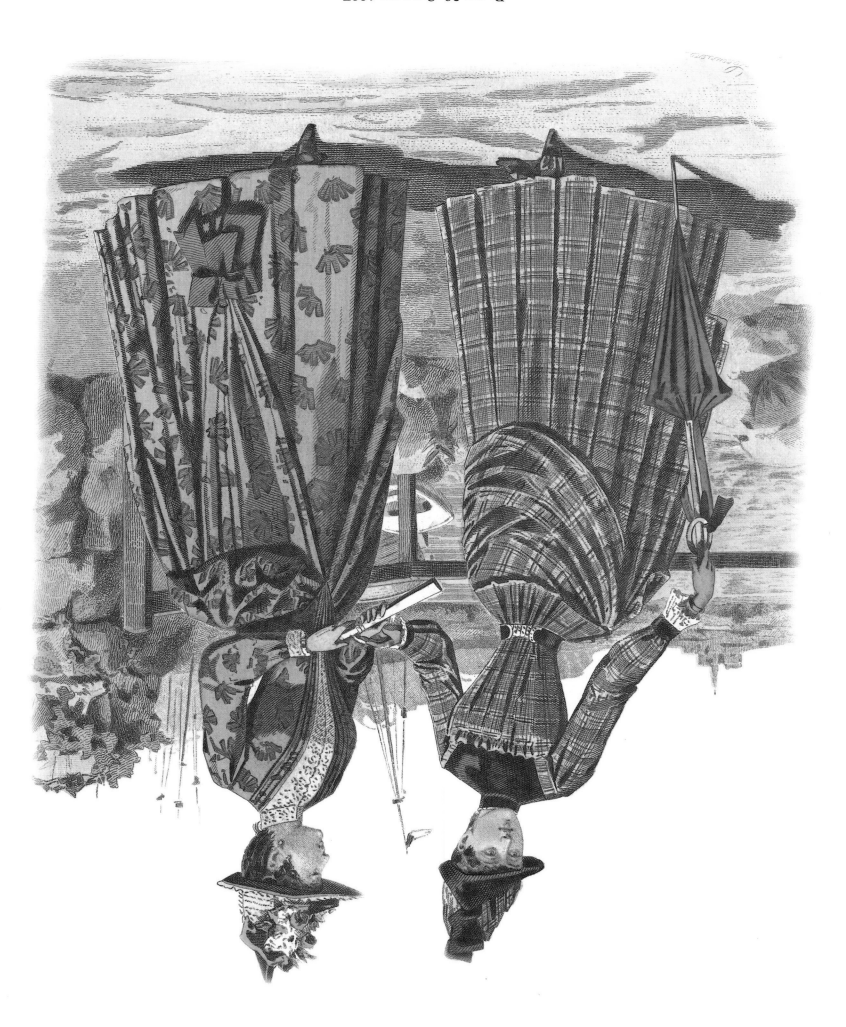

PLATE 31. JULY 1887

PLATE 32. 1887

PLATE 33. SPRING 1887

PLATE 35. FEBRUARY 1888

PLATE 36. DECEMBER 1888

PLATE 37. FALL 1888

PLATE 39. APRIL 1888

PLATE 40. JANUARY-FEBRUARY 1888

PLATE 41. FALL 1888

PLATE 42. SUMMER 1891

PLATE 43. JULY 1891

PLATE 44. FALL 1891

PLATE 45. FALL 1891

Falconer. Imp. Paris

P. Désonville

Esnault

PLATE 46. OCTOBER 1891

Plate 47. Winter 1891

PLATE 48. SEPTEMBER 1892

PLATE 49. JANUARY 1892

PLATE 50. FALL 1893

PLATE 51. 1893

PLATE 52. 1893